Your Free Book

As a way of saying *thanks* for your purchase, I'm offering a free report that's exclusive to my book and my newsletter readers.

In *7 Questions To Build Trust*, you'll discover a ladder of questions that will gain the lasting trust of your team member.

Using these questions you can then follow up to have a truly effective coaching session which will motivate your team like never before.

>>> Go To The Link Below To Claim Your Free Book <<<

www.icaruspublishing.theheasman.com/coaching

Contents

Introduction

As a team leader you want nothing more than to have your team working at their best.

Whether you're in a volunteering organisation, a large corporation, or a start-up, it's common knowledge that when everyone works at their best, everyone gets what they want.

The project gets all the attention and creativity it deserves.

Your customers and clients are more than delighted that you exceed expectations.

You're own manager or whomever you're accountable is pleased at your ability to get so much performance.

Your team soar to new heights and get that psychic reward that comes from completing a challenging project and giving their all.

And finally you're pleased with yourself. Pleased that you were able to bring out the best in your team.

However as you know it's not that simple. If it was a simple case of telling your team *"work your best and you'll be fairly rewarded"*, you wouldn't have picked up this book.

It's often frustrating. You try and seduce that one team member (you know exactly who I'm talking about) with tangible rewards. When that doesn't work you resort to threats and punishment. You see some results, but it doesn't stick.

Sucks right?

You'll be pleased to know this is a common problem.

On leaving University I was thrown in a managerial position in a growing start up.

I was young and cocky enough to believe I had what it takes to make a team perform their best. After all we're all motivated by pleasure gained and pain avoided right? "Use the carrot and stick" we're told.

So I did. And the results were horrible.

I found that when I tried to intervene in this manner the results turned out to be *worse*.

That's right.

When I tried to motivate my employees to perform better, they ended up performing worse.

Suddenly I was not so sure about my job. Here I was fresh out of University and I'm managing employees, and I'm doing a crappy job at it.

I could see where this road was ending.

In my dilemma I did the one thing I was good at as a student: I researched the hell out of the problem.

In the course of my research I found out that the classic "carrot and stick" style of motivation that we're usually taught, doesn't work. That established but often ignored research in social science states that there's actually a *secret* third way to motivate people. A third way that works far better.

I started to use my research. I kept what worked and threw out what didn't.

But…slowly and surely… my team's performance *started* to improve.

I learnt how to address thorny and specific performance issues caused by some members of my team. I learnt how to get them to change their behaviour and for it to actually stick.

After a few months of increased productivity I was able to breathe a sigh of relief. My job was no longer on the line.

After a few more months the CEO congratulated me "Dan...
You turned that team into a bunch of rock stars."

***

In this book you'll find the exact method that I used to coach
my team. The method which unlocked their performance.

You'll learn how to make them superstars in their jobs. How to
make them *love* coming to work in your organisation.

You'll learn how to address thorny performance issues in a
way which won't make people defensive. You'll in fact learn
how to get them on board with making the change.

A quick note, seeing as not everyone works in a corporation I'll
refer to you as the *team leader* and the person you want to
coach as the *team member*. After all not everyone works in a
company, so the labels of *employer, manager* and *employee*
didn't seem appropriate.

If you find this a problem, just replace whenever you see
"team member" with whatever role the person you want to
coach occupies.

Also this book assumes that you have some position of
authority or permission to address performance issues with
your team member. Whether you're in a managerial position,
an employer or you're a consultant brought in to address
performance.

Now seeing as you bought this book, you're probably eager to
coach your team to get them to work at their very best. Or to
fix that niggling issue that's really bothering you.

However before we dive in and show you how to hold an
effective coaching session, we first have to take a little detour
into the tricky subject of motivation...

Chapter 1: Why Motivating Your Employees Doesn't Work, and What Does

So you have a team member who is struggling with your project.

Maybe they don't come into the office on time.

Maybe they don't follow up with their project.

Or maybe you just don't feel like they're giving their all to the work, when you hired them because of the promise they would.

You've probably tried all the classic tips on motivating your team.

You increased the reward for the project, and pointed out to them the benefits to their career (and maybe their purse) if they work on it.

When that didn't work maybe you used the old adage "pain is a better motivator than pleasure" and raised the stakes, stating if they don't fix up they'll undergo a performance review.

But....despite all this it still isn't working.

Otherwise you wouldn't be reading this book.

And the reason for this is simple.

The classic carrot and stick model for motivation doesn't work in a lot of circumstances in the business world.

In fact despite what all the business literature says, social science has shown for the past 50 years that extrinsic motivation isn't enough and in fact harms creativity.

(Extrinsic motivation is when you use external factors to motivate someone. Usually with the threat of punishment, or with the promise of a reward.)

Don't believe me? Let's take a little detour to a certain social science experiment. An experiment involving candles...

The Candle Problem

In the 1930s psychologist Karl Duncker came up with a test used in various experiments in behavioural science called "The Candle Problem".

The experiment is simple. Lying on a table next to a wall is a candle, some matches, and a box of thumbtacks.

The participants are simply asked to attach the candle to the wall using nothing more than these items.

Oh... and the wax can't drip to the table.

And... you have to do this as fast as you can.

Nothing like pressure right?

The participants tried various creative solutions but most of them failed.

Some took a tack and tried to pin the candle to the wall... but that failed.

Some lit a match and melted the wax on the side of the candle and tried to stick it to the wall.... but that failed.

Some however figured out the real solution. It was to empty the box of thumbtacks, stick the box to the wall using some thumbtacks and place the candle inside the box.

The key to solving this problem according to Karl Duncker was overcoming what is called *functional fixedness*.

When you initially see the equipment, you assume each item has one function. It takes some fresh or creative thinking to see that the box that holds the tacks can hold more than one function... that it can be used to hold the candle.

The solution to this problem isn't one of following a set path, but in breaking from tradition and discovering and following a novel strategy.

Sounds like what you want from your team on your project right?

Well this experiment gets more interesting.

In 1962 Professor Sam Glucksberg decided to repeat the experiment but to add a monetary incentive.

This is what all the business management literature says right? People perform in order to maximise wealth. Add incentives and your employees will perform like rock stars.

He devised the test by splitting a set of new participants into new groups.

For Group A he instructed them to solve the Candle Problem. However he told them it would be timed to establish a baseline for how long it takes the average person to solve this puzzle.

Group B on the other hand were incentivised. If a participant's time to solve the puzzle was in the top 25% they would receive $5. If the participant was the fastest of all they would receive $20.

If you adjust those numbers for inflation $5 becomes $40 and $20 becomes $150 in today's money.

Amounts that shouldn't be laughed at for participating in a scientific study.

So how did the experiment turn out? Which group do you expect performed better?

Classic economic thinking would state the second group performed better but Glucksberg found *the exact opposite.*

In fact the second group took on average **three and a half minutes** longer to solve the puzzle.

Oh wait... I forgot. The second group did perform better than the first at one point.

It was when the tacks were taken out of the box. When they didn't have to overcome "functional fixedness".

In other words when no creativity was required, and they simply had to race the finish for a "if, then" task.

So why is this the case? Why did incentives make the second group perform worse in this creative task?

It's been suggested that incentives narrow people's focus. They stop looking for solutions out of the box, as the stakes are real.

Akin to adding blinders to the sides of a horses eyes. It'll race down the track faster, but good luck getting it round an obstacle course.

In case you're thinking that there may be a flaw with this experiment, something which no-one is quite catching, it's been verified twice.

In 2005 Dan Ariely and three other economists representing MIT, Carnegie Mellon and the University of Chicago undertook an experiment commissioned by the Federal Reserve Bank of Boston.

It was similar to Glucksberg work but was performed in Madurai, India where the lower cost of living meant they could offer higher incentives.

Working with eighty-seven participants they asked them to play a series of games and puzzles which tested motor skills, creativity and concentration.

They added variable rewards similar to the Glucksberg experiment of 1962: one-third of the participants could receive a small reward of $0.50 (similar to a day's wage in Madurai) for reaching their targets. Another third could earn a medium reward of $5 (two weeks pay) and another third could earn a large reward of $50 (five months pay).

In the study they found that the highest incentivised group for $50 performed worst of all. In nearly every measure of the experiment they fell behind their medium sized and smaller sized reward cohorts. The researchers concluded:

"In eight of the nine tasks we examined across the three experiments, higher incentives led to worse performance."

Just to re-iterate, this was a study instigated by the Federal Bank of Boston, a subsidiary of one of the holy institutions of capitalism in the U.S, and economists from MIT, Carnegie Mellon and University of Chicago.

Institutions not to be laughed at.

Incentives don't work in motivating employees for creative tasks. In fact it can make them perform worse. Sometimes throwing more money at the problem isn't going to work.

So if incentives don't work, if extrinsic motivation can't make your employees perform their best, what can?

Intrinsic Motivation

It's been found in social science that there is a third form of motivation apart from the carrot and stick.

It's called *intrinsic motivation*.

It's the drive to perform the work for the love of the work itself. The pleasure we take in solving puzzles, or in overcoming a certain challenge.

This *intrinsic motivation* can be separated into three facets: *Autonomy, Mastery, Purpose.*

In a nutshell...

Autonomy

Autonomy provides your team with the creative freedom in how they approach their tasks or their projects. By offering them freedom in the schedule with which they work, how they approach the problem and what work they carry out, you can start to tap into your team member's intrinsic motivation.

A coaching session is key to find out which of these will grant more autonomy to your team member. Some people want more freedom in their schedule. Others like a 9-5, but want more freedom in how they tackle their projects.

In a nutshell try finding out which of these your team members want more of:

Freedom in how they carry out the work: Release restrictions on *how* they complete the task. By all means offer some initial guidance, but let them solve the problem how they see fit, and you may be surprised at the results.

Freedom to work when they want: Instead of restricting the schedule the team member can work, offer a system which only cares about results. It doesn't matter when your team member works, as long as they submit the work on time.

Freedom of what to work on: Consider offering creative time or creative days when they can work on whatever they want. Google is famous for this with their "20% time". Half of Google's new products including Gmail, AdSense and Google News have come from projects birthed during this 20% time.

Mastery

Mastery is basically the process of your team members becoming better at something which matters to them.

A coaching sessions gives you the chance to find out what skills matter to your team member, and which ones they want to develop.

One way to tap into this intrinsic drive with this knowledge is to provide projects and tasks to your employees which are neither too hard nor too simple. Dan Pink, author of *Drive: The Surprising Truth About What Motivates Us*, calls these "Goldilocks tasks". These tasks give your team members the chance to grow, and to avoid boredom.

Also create an environment where mastery is possible. Offer clear goals, immediate feedback and tasks which fall into the "Goldilocks" zone of difficulty.

Purpose

Purpose is self-explanatory. It is the reason you, I and your team members get up in the morning. Everyone has a natural desire to contribute to a greater and more enduring cause than themselves.

A coaching session offers the opportunity to find out what matters to your team members. With this knowledge you can clearly communicate the purpose of your organisation that falls in line with your team member's purpose.

Also the session gives the chance to show your team member that you're all in it together. Use words such as "we" and "us" to show you are on a shared purpose. If you do this right they'll feel part of a greater cause and will become unstoppable.

Autonomy, Mastery & Purpose together add up to explain a person's intrinsic motivation. This is more powerful than using external rewards and punishment to motivate your employees.

Summary:

- In work which requires a little bit of creativity, extrinsic motivators fail to motivate people, in fact it can make them perform worse.
- Intrinsic motivators are much better at motivating people to perform creative tasks.
- A person's intrinsic motivation can be divided into 3 parts: Autonomy, Mastery, Purpose. Provide more of these to a person and they'll become more motivated.

Now that we know what works and what doesn't work in motivating your team, it's time to get to work.

Next up we're going to find out the best strategy to get the most out of your team.

Chapter 2: Why To Coach

It's one thing knowing what intrinsically motivates people. It's another thing putting it into practice.

But how do you do just that?

Or how exactly do you address a specific problem your team member has?

This chapter will show you how.

The Performance Review

Most organisations have a system to ensure performance quality. Most of the time it's a Performance Review.

You probably know of it. You probably have carried out some yourself.

Once a year your team member sits in a room with the team leader and they go through various metrics and projects that have been carried out through the year. The aim is to give constructive feedback the team member can use to improve their performance over the next year.

One day. Out of the three hundred and sixty five days in the year…only one day is spent on assessing performance.

And we expect that to work?

Do you remember College? High School? Do you remember carrying out exams?

You're supposed to spend a few months revising for the exams, but what inevitably happens instead, is that you cram during the weeks following up to the exam. You pull all-nighters, and you binge on more caffeine than is humanly possible.

Come crunch time, you get through the exam, and if you're lucky you get the grade you desire.

You breathe a sigh of relief, knowing that the next time you'll have to push yourself that hard is far off in the distance…in one years' time.

That's the exact kind of behaviour performance reviews promote.

Once a year the team member knows they're going to be assessed. So in the weeks running up to the assessment they improve the quality of their work. They come in on time, they go beyond expectations on the project. They face the performance review, smile and say they'll take on the feedback offered.

And then breathe a sigh of relief they're not going to be under review. They live to fight for another year.

Not exactly a productive attitude is it?

There is another strategy which is more productive. It's more helpful than a performance review. It's the reason you picked up this book.

That's right.

It's Coaching.

Coaching offers a continual feedback cycle with the team member. Instead of bursts of improvement once a year which return to normal, you get a continual trajectory of improvement.

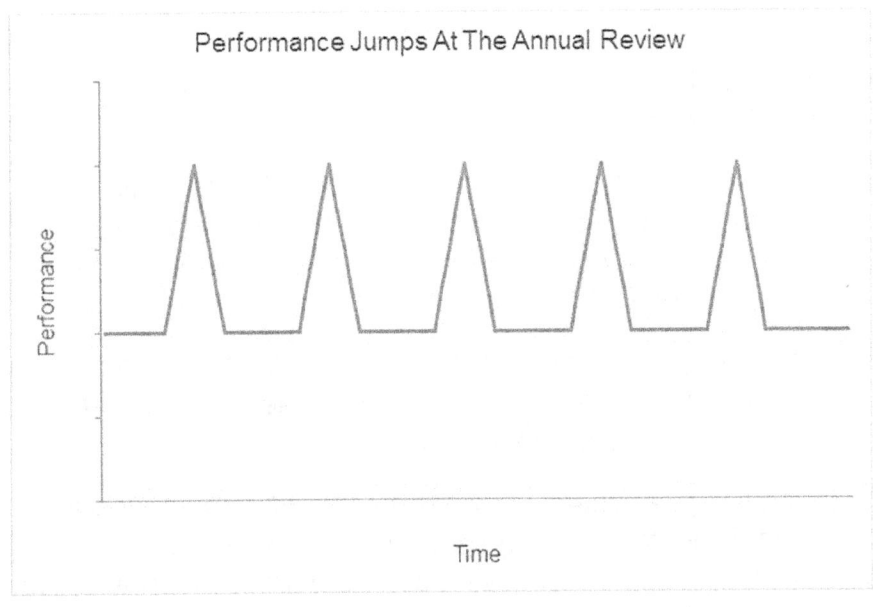

Performance Jumps At The Annual Review

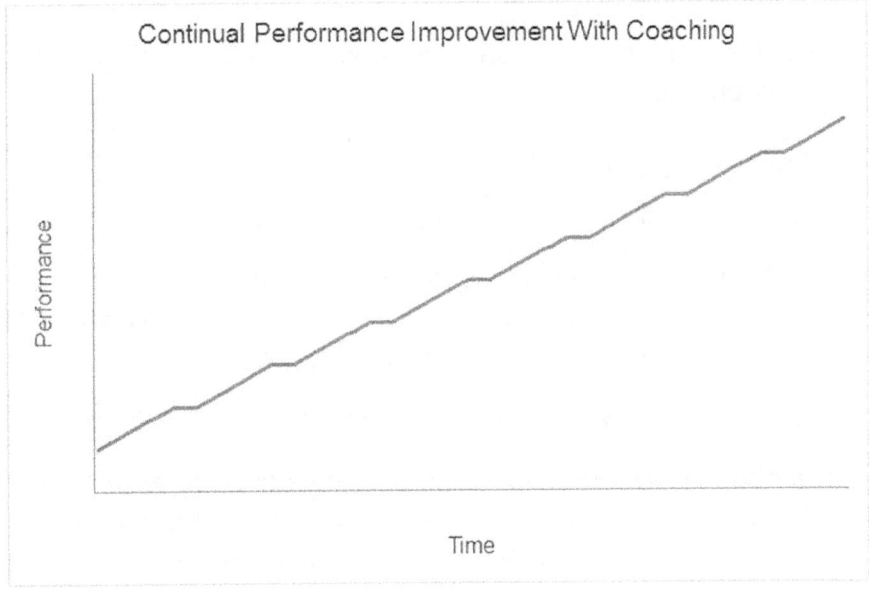

Continual Performance Improvement With Coaching

There are other reasons why if you're not Coaching you're missing out on a strategy which can make your team work more effectively.

Unlock Intrinsic Motivation

As we said before, just knowing what intrinsically motivates people isn't enough to motivate them.

Coaching is the best tool to find out what intrinsically motivates your team members. What exactly do they want to be in *autonomous* in? What exactly do they want to *master*? What *purpose* do they want to contribute to?

Later on in this book I'll show you just how to hold a coaching session to find these out, and how to use this information to motivate your team members.

With a regular coaching sessions the team member can be periodically reminded of these motivators. And any shortcomings they're having can be pointed out in a relaxed, non-threatening environment.

Put it simply, regular coaching sessions will make your team unstoppable.

Address Specific Issues

Perhaps your problem isn't one of motivation.

Perhaps you're having a specific problem with one of your team members. Perhaps they're not giving their all when they used to, or they're consistently making mistakes.

There are two ways to solve this issue:

Hold a meeting with the team member, and tell them what they're doing wrong. Offer them a chance to improve for x reward or if they don't they'll receive y punishment.

As you already know that won't work.

Another way you can address this issue...

Hold a coaching session with the team member. Build trust so they feel comfortable to say what's on their mind. Get them verbally to agree that a performance issue exists. Get them to see the implications of this performance issue. Then explore alternatives of how this issue can be improved. Get a verbal commitment from them to act. Then offer positive feedback.

This way you get the team member on board, getting past any possible resistance and hostility. Also as it's a coaching session, you can use future coaching sessions to assess performance. If they improve, offer positive feedback which will create a positive cycle of improvement. If they don't, a gentle reminder will probably give them the course correct they need.

If you're confused as to how to do that, don't worry I'll show you how to do this later on in the book. The exact way to open the meeting, and the kind of questions to use to build trust and get them on board.

Summary

To conclude Coaching is the most effective strategy to improve your team's performance because:

- Annual Performance Reviews don't encourage continual improvement, while Coaching does.
- Coaching allows you to find your team member's intrinsic motivators.
- Coaching creates an effective environment to get your team member on board to improve a specific performance issue they're lagging on.

Before you can hold a coaching session you need to create an environment which the team member feels comfortable enough to share their intrinsic motivators, and which dispels any hostility.

In other words you need to build trust.

Chapter 3: Building Trust Part 1

So you're ready to coach your team member. Ready to make them unstoppable.

You'll invite them to a meeting and BOOM, you'll coach them and they'll become performance rock stars right?

Well... there's an important step before that.

A step which if you miss out will make the whole effort useless.

It'll be common sense to some of you, but some of you will brush it off.

You see in order to have a truly effective coaching session, the kind which really unlocks your team member's inner drive, and inner enthusiasm to tackle any performance issues...

You have to do something beforehand.

You have to build trust.

Do They Trust You?

In a minute I'll show you effective strategies to build trust and rapport during the coaching session.

But first some of you may think your team already trust you and you can skip this step.

Others of you may think this isn't your role. You're after all the big mean boss, you're team has to fear you, not trust you.

Trust me, you're wrong in both areas.

For an effective coaching session, a trusting atmosphere has to be built.

Here's why.

Imagine for a second you're the team member. Imagine yourself back when you had that role.

Suddenly your team leader calls you in for a meeting or to have a little talk.

What's running through your mind?

First off you're curious what this meeting could be about.

But then something suddenly happens.

The stakes become real. If you lose this job you won't be able to make rent, you won't be able to pay your bills.

You start wondering about what you've done wrong for this meeting to be called. You wonder if **this is it**. The day you've feared will happen.

Maybe you don't go that far, maybe it's not as bad. Maybe the meeting is was called to let you know you're under review. Or maybe that you're not getting that promotion you were hoping for.

Whatever it is, your mind is bracing you for the worst case scenario. Hence when you enter that door you're tense, you're defensive. And if you've got gumption you're going to go down fighting.

Suddenly an innocent meeting can become hostile. Some of the things the team leader says become misinterpreted as your emotions are high, and you read a simple innocent phrase as an attack. You become defensive. You blame another team member, logistics or maybe even the team leader himself.

As you can imagine this atmosphere isn't conducive to a productive coaching session. With this kind of defensiveness there is no way you can address a performance issue without tension, let alone addressing the team member's intrinsic motivation.

This can happen even if your team member trusts you. If they're generally good at their job then they are in fear of losing that job. When people are afraid, fight or flight instincts overtake reason. Words are said, words which can't be taken back.

Hence it is critically important to establish trust and rapport in the beginning of the coaching session. To dispel any fears the team member has.

Why Building Trust Is Important

Another reason to build trust is the topics which are to be covered are a bit sensitive. Whether you're offering some constructive criticism or trying to tap into their intrinsic drive, these matters are a bit personal to the team member.

People don't share their hopes and fears with someone they don't trust.

Often in the workplace people say what they think others want to hear. This isn't a bad thing, as it keeps the environment professional and the business ticking.

But when it comes to a coaching session this is the worst behaviour we can have. If the team member says they're motivated because they love working with the team, but really they're best work happens when they work from the kitchen at home before work, then the entire session has been a loss.

A loss to the organisation and the team member.

You don't want to miss out on increased productivity do you?

Just imagine....one effective coaching session in which you spend just a few minutes, *a few* minutes, in building trust could double your team member's productivity.

What would that be worth to your organisation?

But just in case you don't believe me...

It's been shown that people hold back their feelings and attitudes about an issue if they don't trust the other person.

In a social science study carried out amongst workers in a large US government research laboratory it was found that "The data support the hypothesis that 'a communicator, B, who lacks trust in the recipient of his communication, A, tends to be motivated to conceal his own attitudes about an issue, X, in communicating with A. The accuracy of A's perceptions is impaired accordingly.'"[1]

In other words if there isn't trust between you and your team leader, you'll be receiving false information.

False information which will render the coaching session useless.

A final reason to build trust is because that's the hallmark of a good leader.

You can be feared, but the team still has to trust their leader to get the job done, and to have their backs if everything goes wrong.

If they don't trust you to do that, then they won't perform their best. Period.

Summary

In conclusion it's important to build trust with your team member in the early parts of the coaching session because:

- Building trust will dispel any hostility or defensiveness they've built up before the session.
- If your team member doesn't trust you, he or she won't share what they truly feel about an issue with you. Which would render your coaching session ineffective.
- Intrinsic motivators and criticism are sensitive topics to people. You're only going to get what they *really* feel if they trust you.

Now that you know that building trust is important, we're going to get to the good stuff. We're going to show you exactly how to build trust.

Chapter 4: Building Trust Part 2

In this chapter we're going to get straight to it.

We're going to show you how to build trust during your coaching session so that your team member can open up, get on board with addressing a performance issue, or share their intrinsic motivators.

Let's get to it.

Don't Move On Until You've Done This

There is one thing you HAVE to do before you get into the coaching session.

Do not pass GO, do not collect $200. Go straight to this.

Don't even think of holding a coaching session or asking questions before you do this:

As you begin the meeting make it clear to the team member they are not in trouble, and that you just want to talk.

Before the meeting is scheduled, the team member is going to be nervous, apprehensive and potentially hostile about the meeting. People fear the unknown, and they're mind will have started running into worst case scenarios.

Begin the meeting by dispelling these fears, and you're well on your way to the relaxed and trusting atmosphere required for an effective coaching session.

Establish Common Ground

In 1914 out on the western front during World War I, the British and the Germans had been waging a long and bloody conflict outside Ypres, Belgium.

The horrors of trench warfare aside, World War I was one of the bloodiest wars ever fought, with the machine gun being used with devastating effect by the Germans.

To hear the call "to go over the top" and to charge the enemy amidst a shower of machine gun fire was a death sentence to many British soldiers.

As you can imagine, the Brits didn't exactly feel too fond of their German counterparts at the time.

However on December 24th the British soldiers began to hear songs and see some lights coming from the opposite side's trenches which lay across the field separating them.

As the British soldiers listened more, they recognised that the songs were in fact Christmas carols, and the lights were candles lit to celebrate Christmas.

Then...something unprecedented and amazing happened.

The two opposing armies which had been fighting and killing each other for months and months on end, came out of their trenches and began to celebrate Christmas together.

They sang carols, shared trinkets and family photos in complete trust that no killing would occur. There was even a bit of healthy competition in the form of a football match.

It's a touching Christmas story...but how? How did this happen?

How did men who had been killing each other for months on end, trust each other enough to celebrate and not kill each other for one day?

No-one knows for certain, but David Desteno a Professor of Psychology has a simple theory.

"...I suspect that it was because in those moments, the men stopped viewing themselves as British and Germans, and

rather saw themselves as fellow Christians. They came to perceive themselves as similar, and that meant they could trust each other."[2]

What does this have to do with you building trust?

It's simple.

During your coaching session find things which both of you share, whether it be interests, demographics or circumstantial position. Anything which can be perceived as both of you belonging to something similar.

Once you've found some things, naturally emphasise them. Be natural about it. Drop it casually in conversation, but continue to emphasise it.

If you do it correctly your team member will see you have things in common and slowly warm to you and trust you enough to start opening up.

However be careful. Exercise your people skills. Don't be *too* overt or ingenuous in your emphasis. Otherwise your team member will realise what you're doing and shut down. No-one likes to feel like they're being manipulated.

And you'll be surprised just how good we are at picking up people who are ingenuous.

Change Your Language

Similar to before, you want to listen to the kind of words your team member uses.

A simple neuro-linguistic programming trick is to find out how someone processes information. Using this you can break people into three different types of character: *visual* thinkers, *aural* thinkers and *kinaesthetic* thinkers.

For example,

"I **see** what you're saying...I think we should..."

"I *hear* what you're saying...I think we should..."

"I *feel* what you're saying....I think we should...."

The first clearly shows someone who thinks in visual terms, the second thinks in aural terms, and the final person thinks in kinaesthetic terms.

Most people you'll meet are visual thinkers, but every so often you'll meet someone who's an aural thinker and occasionally someone who thinks kinaesthetically. The idioms as well as the language they'll use will change accordingly. For example.

- Visual: *"Yes I get the picture."*
- Aural: *"That rings a bell."*
- Kinaesthetic: *"This is a rough patch we're going through"*

Once you've identified the manner in which they process information, shift your language to be in a similar manner. If they're visual say "I see" to agree with what they're saying. Adjust if they're aural or kinaesthetic thinkers.

This builds trust on an unconscious level and ties in with what we said earlier. People trust people who they perceive as similar to them.

Honesty is the Best Policy
Whenever possible be honest.

Yes, I know this sounds hooey, but it's important. White lies are important for social cohesion, but in the coaching session a white lie can be pretty damaging.

As any five year old will tell you, you win trust by being honest.

However this is a hard habit to kick.

A study by the University of Massachusetts found that 6 out of 10 adults couldn't have a ten minute conversation without at least telling one lie.[3]

However white lies can build upon each other until slowly an atmosphere of distrust grows in an office environment.

I'm not asking you to stop lying. That would be nearly impossible. But at least during the coaching session leave your white lies at the door. If something comes up which you're not comfortable telling the entire truth about, simply deflect.

They'll get that you don't want to talk about it and move on.

Damaging Admission

This is the final arsenal in your toolkit to build trust. And it's one everyone knows but many use wrongly.

And that is... to make a damaging admission.

This is simply admitting something which could potentially damage your character. A mistake you've made in the past, or something you're struggling with.

When done right, damaging admissions are a natural way to build trust. However too many people abuse them.

Trust me on this, your team member will know when you're being ingenuous about your damaging admission.

So how do you do it naturally?

Well during the coaching session if the team member is struggling with a performance issue, maybe share a time in the past you've made a mistake. Or a time you were struggling with something similar.

You're human, I'm pretty sure you've made mistakes. Why not use them to build trust?

If it's regarding intrinsic motivation, get your team member on board by sharing a time when you were struggling with being motivated.

Again…you're human. I'm pretty sure there were times when you were unmotivated for your job. Why not use this as fuel to build trust?

Your team member will naturally trust you if they know you've been in a similar situation. They'll also be more agreeable to sharing what they're having trouble with and willing to address the issue.

If you use damaging admissions correctly, you'll open up a healthy and honest dialogue during the coaching session, paving the pathway to success.

Summary

To conclude you can build trust with your team member during the coaching session by:

- Dispelling any nerves or hostility by telling them upfront that they're not in trouble and you just want to talk. Don't move on until you've done this.
- During the session identify anything you have in common with your team member and emphasise this naturally.
- Identify whether they're a visual, aural, or kinaesthetic thinker by the language they use. Then shift the words you use to match their style.
- Be honest during the coaching session and avoid the temptation to tell any white lies.
- Use a damaging admission that's relevant to the topic of the coaching session to open an honest dialogue. However ensure this is done naturally and genuinely. People can detect when it's done ingenuously.

Now that you know how to build trust, we'll show you how exactly to begin the coaching session so that both you and your team member can get the most out of it.

Chapter 5: How To Begin A Coaching Session

So you now know why coaching is important, what drives people, and even how to build trust.

You're eager to fire up your interpersonal skills, start coaching your team, and get superstar performance.

But you may be wondering....

"Just how the hell do I start a coaching session?"

If that's the case. Relax. In this chapter I'm going to show you the exact logistics to starting a coaching session.

Before we get into it though, it'll help if you know the different stages to a coaching session.

Whether you're addressing a specific performance issue, or trying to tap into your team member's intrinsic motivation, the coaching session follows the same format.

So without further ado...

The 7 Steps to a Successful Coaching Session

Step 1 Build Trust

As we've talked before building trust is essential for both you and the team member to get anything out of a coaching session. Building trust doesn't just happen inside the coaching session, it also happens outside. During your day to day interactions with your team.

If you follow the steps from the previous chapter, especially the one of being honest and transparent, and having your team's back, then this stage is a walk in the park.

Step 2 Open The Meeting

Remember what I said was very essential in the previous chapter?

Of dispelling any fears the team member has about the meeting?

Well that's what this step is about.

As well as initiating the meeting, you should make it clear to the team member that they're not in trouble and that you just want to have a talk.

I'll show you exactly how to do this later on in the chapter.

Step 3 Get Agreement

After a bit of small talk during the early stages of the meeting, where you establish an atmosphere of trust, perhaps you've found some common interests or links with the team member to slowly build trust, you need to then get agreement from the team member.

The key here is to ask in a non-judgemental way whether the team member agrees there is a performance issue, whether something specific or that of motivation.

It helps if you clearly define what the issue is and bring it up with the team member. Maybe cite previous examples of the behaviour that's causing the issue, and make the team member clearly see the implications and consequences of this behaviour. Not only to the organisation, but to the team, and to themselves.

Remember to do this in a non-judgemental way. Perhaps this may be a good time to share a previous example of a mistake you made in your past. As a team leader it's expected that you have a few war stories of your own.

When addressing the implications and consequences the key isn't to "preach it" but to ask questions to probe what the team member understands about the consequences of the performance issue.

This philosophy of asking questions during a coaching session will be talked about in a later chapter, as well what questions to ask.

Step 4 Explore Solutions

Now that both you and the team member agree that a problem exists, it's time to explore alternative methods to arrive at a solution.

If you're addressing intrinsic motivation this is the part where you would ask questions to find out what kind of autonomy they desire on a project, what kind of skills they want to improve and what greater cause is close to their hearts.

Using this information it'll be up to you as the team leader to find solutions which converge with the team members intrinsic drivers. What can you be flexible on regarding autonomy? What projects can they work on that will grow the skills they want to master? What aspects and values of your organisation converge with your team member's values?

Yes it isn't easy, but that's *why you're the team leader*. It's in the job description. Leading isn't all about telling people what to do. It's about facilitating your team to deliver on the project.

If however you're not addressing intrinsic motivation but a specific performance issue, this is where you explore alternatives the team member could do which would address the issue. Maybe they change their routine, or their work habits.

It's important that **both of you** come up with a number of solutions, not just the ones you've thought of. Now that the team member is on board, you may be surprised at the solutions your team member comes up with. After all they know themselves best.

After you've come up with a wealth of solutions, and you've discussed the pros and cons of each, it's time to...

Step 5 Get Commitment

This step is all about getting the team member to commit to act on one of the alternatives discussed. It's also for you to commit to act on whatever you can do on your end, whether it's shifting them onto another project, or making a new tool available to them.

To complete this step both of you have to get verbal agreement from each other. Agreement on what action they're going to take from now on.

Remember this is a *coaching session*, so be sure to support whatever choice the team member makes, and offer genuine and specific praise.

Step 6 Handle Objections

During the coaching meeting objections or excuses may crop up from the team member.

After all you're addressing things which are somewhat personal to the team member. People tie up their self-identity with their performance.

When an objection or an excuse comes up, chances are it's because the team member perceived a statement or comment as an accusation.

Here you should rephrase the statement that was perceived wrongly and re frame it as encouragement for the team member to examine their own behaviour. After all your team member wants to grow, and we grow by improving our behaviour.

Also throughout show that you understand where the team member is coming from and that you empathise with their situation.

Step 7 Provide Feedback

The final part of the coaching session. It's an ongoing process and continues outside of the session.

It's simple: if you don't give feedback, the change won't stick.

Give continual performance to your team member on a regular basis. It should be positive and correct any flaws that are critical.

When giving feedback make sure that it's:

- **Timely:** As soon as it's possible after the session, give feedback. Whether it's on completion of a task that was agreed upon or you observe the change.
- **Don't be vague**: Avoid using vague statements such as "great job" or "you didn't make the customer happy". Instead be specific on the behaviour you want changed. "I liked how you handled the client's initial objections during the call" or "next time why don't you try using this tone of voice on the phone."
- **What" not "Why":** Avoid sounding judgemental. This is easily done if you focus on what the team member is doing, as opposed to why you think they're doing it. Beginning with statements such as "I've observed...." and "I've seen...." set you up in good stead. Using "I've noticed..." will likely end up with you making a character statement as opposed to a behaviour statement, which the team member will take as an accusation.
- **Encouraging tone of voice:** If not encouraging, at least sincere. Avoid sounding angry, exasperated or sarcastic.

We'll go more into these stages later on in the book. But for now that's a brief overview of a successful coaching session.

How To Begin The Session

Now that you have a general idea of the coaching session, it's time to show you how to begin the session.

If you do this part right, you'll start the session with an atmosphere of trust and openness, which will get your team member more readily on board, making it easier to address any issues.

If you do this part wrong, the team member will be nervous, defensive and perhaps hostile.

An opportunity to improve performance quickly becomes a shouting match with words said that can't be taken back.

I don't need to tell you that the resulting atmosphere of distrust will harm performance.

I'm sure you want to avoid that right?

Good.

Now let's show you how to start a coaching session.

Arrange And Schedule The Meeting.

Arrange beforehand, ideally a day before or a few hours before, a meeting with the team member. Tell them you want to have a chat. Avoid making it sound formal.

Of course I don't need to tell you that you should arrange for the talk to happen somewhere private. Find a room and book it. If it's appropriate maybe have the talk over coffee.

Clarify That It's Non Judgemental & Non Evaluative

As I've said a few times already, when you begin the meeting or if the team member nervously asks you what the meeting is about, make it clear to them that it's just a talk and they're not in trouble. Emphatically state that it's not an evaluation, and you just want to talk about how they've been performing at work.

Again at the risk of sounding repetitive tell them they're not in trouble.

Establish An Atmosphere Of Trust

During the opening stages of the session engage in some small talk. Use your common sense and some tips from the previous chapter to build an open atmosphere of trust. The key is to show that inside the session is a safe place. You'll offer no judgemental criticisms on anything they say.

If you do this right you'll have set the stage for an effective and successful coaching session. The next parts will come easier as a result.

Summary

To summarise it's important to begin the coaching session right:

- Recall the 7 stages to a coaching session.
- Invite the team member to have a talk.
- When opening the meeting, make sure to tell the team member they're not in any trouble.
- Using your common sense and tips from the previous chapter establish an atmosphere of trust in the opening parts of the session.

With this atmosphere of trust, you're now ready to get to the meaty part of the session. You're going to learn the power of questions, and how to use them to really dig deep, and unlock your team's performance.

Chapter 6: What Questions To Ask

So you've started the coaching session. You've established an atmosphere of trust.

What do you do now?

Well wouldn't it be great if there was a method which thoroughly involved the team member?

A method which made the team member form their own arguments for why they're not performing as well as they could…A method which made the team member convince themselves that they need to change…

All without you needing to say that much…

Wouldn't that be great?

Well I'm here to tell you that there is such a thing.

It's a pretty simple method.

All you have to do is **ask the team member questions**. That's it.

The Power of Questions

When we're convinced of something, when we have the desire to persuade and convince someone of something, we tend to fall into a pattern.

It's a pattern that's been conditioned into us by society.

And that is to pitch. To pitch and preach what we believe. To pitch our conviction, and if our conviction is strong enough, our arguments valid, then people will listen. Then they will be persuaded.

I'm here to tell you that this is simply not true.

The world's best salesmen know this.

The world's greatest philosophers know this.

Preaching doesn't work, questions do.

Why?

There's a subtle power in using questions. When you ask someone something, they immediately evaluate the answer. If you ask the right questions, they'll start to see the merits of what you're leading to through their own arguments. In effect they'll convince themselves of what you're trying to argue.

Socrates knew this. He was the inventor of the technique known as the Socratic dialogue. When Socrates made an argument, he would do it through a series of questions with his adversary about their point of view. They would be simple questions, to which the adversary would offer his simple answers. In doing this Socrates would find out more about the adversary's arguments.

After a few more questions, Socrates would detect a flaw, and he would ask a few more questions which would force the adversary to contradict themselves. He would then point out the contradiction, and through a few more questions the adversary would be forced to admit they were wrong.

So effective was Socrates at this that he was eventually imprisoned and forced to drink poison. It seems his questions made some Athenians very uncomfortable. But that's another story.

Of course I'm not suggesting you should ask questions to the point where you're forced to drink hemlock, but there is a power in using questions.

Sales

So effective are questions that the best salesmen know this.

When it comes to selling high ticket equipment and services, the best salesmen know that pitching the benefits of their equipment won't be enough.

In *Spin Selling* Neil Rackham found through analysing 35,000 different sales calls that the very best salesmen would first ask questions to make the prospect admit the problems they were having with their existing solution.

Then they would ask questions which would make the prospects realise the implications of these problems, making them see that they're far larger than they'd initially thought. Finally after all this, they would ask questions to make the prospects see just how beneficial solving those implications would be to them.

To put it simply questions persuade. Preaching makes people shut down.

So are you willing to find out how to ask questions?

To find out the right kind of questions to get your team member to open up? The kind of questions that will determine their intrinsic motivation? The kind of questions that will get them to admit the problem?

If so, good. Let's get to it.

Questions to determine Intrinsic Motivation

With these questions the key is to find out what the team member would want to be more autonomous in, what they want to master, and what purpose would drive them. If you get these right, you're team member will give you answers which you can use to make them perform like superstars.

Questions to determine Autonomy:

- *What has been the most exciting work experience for you this month?*

Listen to the answer they give, chances are they'll tell you what the task is about, but what you really want to find out are the circumstances surrounding the task.

Follow up with questions such as:

- *Who were you working with on this project?*

This will tell you if there are any other team members who they get on well with, who bring out the best in them. If possible, consider teaming them together more often.

- *Did you carry out any of the work from home?*

If they say yes to this, ask them to give a rough percentage of how much work they got home compared to how much they did in the office. If your team member gets more work done from home, consider how it would be possible in your environment to facilitate this more.

- *Why was this experience exciting for you?*

This is probably the most important question to follow up with. If your team member trusts you enough they'll tell you exactly what it was about the project that brought out the best in them. If however they don't trust you, they'll tell you what they think you want to hear.

This is why building trust in the earlier stages is really important.

Questions to determine Mastery.

These questions are to find out what skills which when practised by your team member, make them work at their best.

The earlier question of "*why was this experience exciting for you?*" may bring some answers that shed some light on this area. However if they don't, these questions should help.

- *Do you consider your current role as your ideal job? What could you be doing that would benefit the business more - and make the experience more enjoyable for you as well?*

Again if you've built trust, then this is a POWERFUL question. Here your team member will tell you whether they like the skills they're exercising in their current role. If not it gives them an opportunity to share a few ideas that they're passionate about.

How much would it be worth to your team and your organisation if you're team member is passionate about what they're doing?

Exactly.

Follow up with any questions you have about their ideas and what it is about practising those skills which will bring their best to the table.

Questions to determine Purpose.

These questions are to determine what reason galvanises the best in your team member. And how you can bridge them with your company's own vision and values.

- *Do you feel like you get a sense of purpose from our mission and vision? If not, tell me what gives you purpose?*

Sometimes the team member will be completely in line with your company's vision. However sometimes they won't. A good follow up question to get them thinking how their purposes align would be:

- *How could you leverage that mission for our organisation?*

Your team member will come up with a few ideas, explore them together with them.

These questions are meant to be a guide. No conversation is scripted, so feel free to switch these questions to make them more appropriate for your unique situation.

Also if you think a different follow up question will get you to your team member's intrinsic motivators during your session, go with it. The key is to find out what autonomy drives your team member, what skills bring out their best, and what mission gets them up in the morning. If you come up with questions that you feel will be better at getting these answers, then feel free to use them. You know your situation better than anyone else.

But what about if you don't want to address your team member's intrinsic motivators?

What about if you want to address a particular performance issue?

The next section is for you.

Questions to address a performance issue.

In the third step of the coaching session, the goal is to get agreement from your team member that a performance issue exists.

It helps if you have the performance issue defined in your own mind. Simply trying to address the fact that they're "not working hard enough" or that they're "lazy" will not do anyone any favours.

If however for example they keep forgetting to use a certain system, if they keep making the same mistakes, and you've defined this as the issue, then you're well on your way to an effective coaching session.

A good question to ask to get the conversation rolling is:

- *How do you feel about your performance in _____?*

Or

- *How do you feel about use of _____?*

Where you fill in the blanks with whatever is appropriate.

Your team member may admit a performance issue exists with their answer. However if they don't, a good follow up strategy is to:

- Tell them a specific example of the performance issue.
- Make clear to them the performance expectations in this area.
- Ask them if they agree.

If they're stubborn or fail to agree, keep citing more and more examples of the performance issue. Overwhelming evidence tends to make people agree.

If they make objections or excuses, it's because they've taken what you've said as an accusation. Re-frame the statement they perceived as accusatory into encouragement for the team member to examine their own behaviour.

Once you've gotten agreement from the team member the next step is to get them to understand the implications of this performance issue. The consequences it has on the business, the team or the project.

A good question for this is:

- *Why do you think it is important that you get _____ right?*

From there ask more probing questions to draw out the team member's understanding of the consequences. Clarify gently if they're mistaken about something.

Questions to explore alternative solutions

Once you've gotten agreement from the team member that a performance issue exists, the next step is to explore alternatives with them.

In order to keep the team member on board it's key to get them to offer some of their own ideas for alternative solutions.

Good questions to start this idea generation process are:

- *How could you do _____ better?*
- *What could be changed about _____?*
- *Instead of using _____ what could you use instead?*

Offer encouragement to any ideas they come up, and offer some of your own. Go through the advantages of each and disadvantages of each.

If this part is done right, you're well on the way to addressing and improving the performance issue. The next steps are simply to decide on a solution and get a verbal commitment to act from the team member. From there with a bit of positive feedback and corrections done in a positive manner, you'll make the behaviour change stick.

Summary

In summary:

- Asking questions is more powerful than telling, pitching or preaching in changing people's behaviour.
- Good questions to find out what autonomy drives your team member are *"What has been the most exciting work experience for you this month?", "Who were you working with on this project?", "Did you carry out any of the work from home?", "Why was this experience exciting for you?"*
- A good question to find out what skill your team member is driven to master is, *"Do you consider your current role as your ideal job? What could you be doing that would benefit*

the business more - and make the experience more enjoyable for you as well?"

- A great way to find your team member's purpose and how it can align with your organisation's mission is to ask, *"Do you feel like you get a sense of purpose from our mission and vision? If not, tell me what gives you purpose?"* followed by *"How could you leverage that mission for our organisation?"*

- If you want to address a performance issue, use questions such as *"How do you feel about your performance in _____?"*, or *"How do you feel about use of _____?"* to get agreement from them.

- Once you've gained agreement ask *"Why do you think it is important that you get _____ right?"* to get your team member's understanding of the consequences of the performance issue.

- Once they've agreed to the consequences ask questions such as *"How could you do _____ better?"*, *"What could be changed about _____?"*, *"Instead of using _____ what could you use instead?"* to get them to list alternative solutions.

It's one thing knowing the questions to ask, however another critical component of a coaching session is knowing how to listen. If you don't listen to the answers your team members give effectively, then the coaching session will be a bust.

Next up we'll show you just how to listen, so that your team member isn't scared to share the truth with you.

Chapter 7: How To Listen Effectively

By now you've built a trusting atmosphere, and you've asked your team member some questions to get the coaching session going.

However you have to do something else effectively or those questions are useless.

You have to listen in the right way.

If you fail to do this, then you will completely torpedo the coaching session.

An Attentive Listener

Do you remember the last time you shared a story with someone?

How did you feel as you shared the story?

Did you feel great, or did you feel frustrated?

Chances are if you felt great it was because you had an attentive listener.

If you felt the other way it was because you had an inattentive listener. Perhaps they weren't all there. Perhaps they kept interrupting, or maybe they were checking their phone, clearly not giving you any attention.

A lousy listener makes for lousy sharing.

The whole purpose of this coaching session is to get the team member on board with a change in their performance. Whether it's to increase their intrinsic motivation or to address a thorny performance issue.

If you don't listen with 100% of your attention the team member will know, and they'll feel unappreciated as they share their answers with you. This will cause them to not be as open with your next question.

If you do listen with 100% of your attention however.... something amazing will happen.

There is a certain magic in having an attentive listener. It builds trust between the teller and the listener. It makes people feel appreciated.

As Dale Carnegie said in his classic book *How To Win Friends and Influence People,*

"If you want people to like you, Rule 1 is:

Become Genuinely Interested In Other People."

Don't Interrupt

When your team member is sharing their answers or their thoughts to a question you asked them, you'll feel tempted to interrupt. Maybe to offer a comment, a slight criticism, or a slight judgement call.

Ignore this temptation.

No really. If you want this coaching session to be productive, DON'T interrupt the team member when they're talking.

Don't criticise, or offer feedback. Listen to what they're saying attentively. Withhold the impulse to cut in with what's on your mind.

Criticisms and unwarranted interruptions are the biggest killers of productive Coaching sessions.

Don't worry, there will be a chance to offer feedback later. And when you do, it will be far more effective than if you butted in right there and then.

After all you want to see an improvement in performance right?

So practice some self-control and don't butt in. There'll be time for that later.

Don't Take Notes

You'll also think it would be helpful to take notes while listening to the team member during the coaching session.

Don't.

There are two reasons for this:

- Taking notes makes the team member feel like they're being judged. If they feel judged they'll tell you what they think you want to hear, as opposed to what they really think. This will make the coaching session useless.
- If you're taking notes, it means you're not fully paying attention. You need to be 100% with them when they're talking. Listening to what they're saying, trying to get the nuance and the context behind their answer.

If you think you can get on the same page as someone by not fully paying attention, good luck. No really...you're going to need it with that attitude.

But if you fully pay attention, you'll get more insights into the team member. The team member will feel great after the session, and is more likely to stick to the change that will be discussed.

As Seth Godin says:

"Ask an entrepreneur leaving the office of a great VC (Venture Capitalist) like Fred Wilson. She'll tell you that she gave the best pitch of her career - largely because of the audience. The hardest step in better listening is the first one: do it on purpose. Make the effort to actually be good at it."[4]

Don't worry about taking notes or summarising what they're saying. You can do that later, at the end of the session.

The important parts will stick with you long enough for to write them down half an hour later.

How To Listen

Once you've asked a team member a question here is how to listen effectively:

- Write down beforehand a list of things you want to say or questions to ask. This brain dump will relieve the mental burden of you thinking of what to say next, freeing you up to mindfully listen to the team member.
- Make sure you're not taking notes. Pay attention to the words the team member is saying.
- Maintain eye contact where possible with the team member.
- You'll be tempted to filter and judge what the other person is saying based on your experiences and assumptions. Don't. Listen fully. Really feel what they're saying. Don't brush off any information they offer. You'll find some nuggets of information.

A study in 2011 by the *Organizational Behaviour and Human decision Processes* found that the more powerful the listener, the more likely he is to judge or dismiss advice from others.[5]

You're the team leader so you're in a position of power. Ignore the temptation to judge or dismiss what the team member is saying.

- Listen with enthusiasm. Use verbal nods such as "hmmm" or "ah" or "yeah". Where possible summarise what they're saying and give them the nod to go on.

Listening is important. A 2007 study of over 3,000 workers in the Academy of Management Journal concluded that employees who don't believe their boss are listening to them are less likely to offer helpful suggestions and new ideas.

How useful would one really good idea be to your organisation in a year?

Isn't it worth turning off your presumptions and really listening to maybe get that one good idea?

Now that you're really listening to your team member, it's time to give you the reward. It's time to show you how to effectively give feedback in a way which the team member will listen to and take action on.

Chapter 8: How To Give Feedback

Finally... you've heard what your team member has to say in regards to your questions.

You've gotten agreement from them an issue exists.

And you have some ideas on feedback to give.

There's only a problem.

You've given feedback to a team member before, and they didn't follow through.

It might have been this team member, it might have been at a different organisation.

You know that not everyone takes on board the feedback they're given.

So how can you get the team member to listen to what you have to say and take action with it?

Don't Tell

It's pretty simple.

If you just tell them the feedback you have on your mind, the reason what they're doing isn't working and what they should do, chances are they won't listen to you.

People don't listen when they feel like they're being judged. Not unless the stakes are really high.

If there is any hint of judgement or criticism in your feedback, the team member's hackles are going to go up

Suddenly their ego is on the line. Their back is against the wall, and they're going to defend their position no matter what you say.

Any trust you've built up during the session will rapidly fade away, and you'll have an unproductive argument on your hands.

There's a simple alternative to this.

Power negotiators and successful salesmen know this.

It's called the *"Feel, felt, found"* strategy to address something.

When the team member has offered something you think that needs chancing, you first **feel** what they're saying such as "I understand....", "I get.....", "I feel....."

Then you follow up with "others have **felt** the same way...." or "Jim the other day was telling me the exact same thing..."

Then you conclude with what they've **found.** This is your chance to give feedback, "however they've **found** that if they use the new system they save 20% of their wasted time," or "but when Jim **found** out what HR have to go through, he changed his tune..."

A few more examples:

"I completely *understand* where you're coming from. Some of my previous clients have *felt* the same way. However they *found* that our 24 hour customer service is exactly that: 24 hours."

"I totally *get* what you're saying, others have been *saying* the same things for years, however they've *found* that...."

When you have something to offer at the end of the session use *feel, felt, found* to soften the sting of what you're saying. This way any defensiveness the team member feels will be dispelled, and they'll take on board what they're saying.

Intrinsic Motivation

Regarding intrinsic motivation, it's up to you and your creativity to come up with a way in which your organisations values align with the team members values. Also if there's any room for flexibility in the projects you can give the team member and any autonomy you can give, you'll be able to get the team member on board with any changes you want them to make.

Performance Issue

If addressing a specific performance issue, then follow the 7 stage strategy shown in Chapter Five: How To Begin A Coaching Session.

Stage 1: Schedule the meeting

Stage 2: Build Trust

Stage 3: Get Agreement

Stage 4: Explore Alternatives

Stage 5: Get a Verbal Commitment to Act

Stage 6: Address objections and excuses

Stage 7: Give Positive Feedback.

Throughout both coaching sessions ensure you use *feel, felt, found* as much as possible when giving feedback.

Chapter 9: Mistakes To Avoid

So you now know an overview of how to coach.

However there are pitfalls along the way which will derail your coaching session.

They are common mistakes, and they are easy to avoid.

So without further ado here are a list of common mistakes new coaches make.

And how to avoid them.

Avoid Failing To Follow Up and Holding Regular Coaching Sessions.

Many new team leaders who use this coaching strategy to address a team member's performance or to improve their intrinsic motivation make a critical mistake.

They think that the work is done once the coaching session is over.

This is far from the truth.

In order to get the changes that you want to stick, you have to offer feedback in a timely fashion.

Reinforce it when the team member delivers a result that's in line with what you agreed by specifically praising them.

And don't hold these sessions only once a year.

That's a sure way to miss out on making your team members perform like rock stars.

Hold them on a semi regular schedule. Maybe once every 2 months, or more regularly if it's appropriate.

Avoid Failing to Listen Effectively

This is a common mistake, and it's not surprising.

Most people have bad listening habits. Prejudging what they hear based on their pre-existing assumptions, hurrying to finish the sentence or the stream of thought, or just the simple fact they easily lose attention.

And this is usually fine. After all we're not graded on our listening ability in life.

However the coaching session is the ONE place where you are graded on your listening ability.

If you fail to listen attentively to the team member, they will know, and the coaching session will become a waste of time.

Avoid Failing to Build a Trusting Environment

Many team leaders assume that their team trusts them and thinks they can skip this step.

However this does more harm than good.

It's not a reflection on your ability as a team leader if your team don't trust you enough to share their intrinsic motivations, or their real thoughts regarding their performance.

This is perfectly natural in the professional environment. Many people have worked in environments where sharing what they really think, even in confidence, can affect their job security.

In other words, say what you really think about the new system and you get fired.

And even if they haven't, everyone knows someone who has suffered that fate.

Because of this you should assume that no matter what you've been through as a team, you still have to build trust before the coaching session.

Think about it not as more a matter of building trust, but as a matter of building and communicating that this is a safe environment for the team member to say what they really think. Nothing said in the room will be judged or criticised.

Avoid Failing To Address Intrinsic Motivation

Many intangible performance problems are actually symptoms of a larger problem.

There's a quote which was popularised in Victor Frankl's *Man's Search For Meaning*:

> "*He who has a why to live can bear almost any how.*" – Friedrich Nietzsche

Cheesy…but true.

We spent a lot of time going through intrinsic motivation in this book, because if you address and improve this, many other performance problems either improve or just fade away.

To put it another way, intrinsic motivation is the drug cocktail to make your team perform like rock stars.

If you address this, if you find out what intrinsically motivates your employees as we showed you, and you align your work situation to fit…. the results will surprise you.

So before addressing a specific symptom, perhaps try seeing if there is a root cause you can address. The root cause of intrinsic motivation.

Conclusion

Well there you have it.

You now know everything you need to unlock the inner rock star in your team.

I assure you if you follow what you've just learnt you'll see results.

You know why coaching is important and what really drives people, and how to use that to get your team to fall in love with working in your organisation.

You know that building trust is important, and you know exactly how to build trust.

You know the power of asking questions and what questions to ask to find out what you want, and to get the team member to convince themselves of your own point of view.

You know just how important listening attentively is and how to do it.

And finally you know exactly how to give feedback in a non-judgemental manner in which your team member will actually take your advice on board and run with it.

All in all you know a lot more than other team leaders in how to unlock the inner rock star in your team.

And that's why you picked up this book. You want to see the performance of your team improve.

Only you can judge how important that is to you. Whether it's because your job is on the line, or because you want that promotion. Or maybe because you just want to be a better leader.

Now it's up to you. All the knowledge I've shown you is just that: knowledge.

You need to take action on what you've learnt, otherwise this knowledge will be a waste of time.

Think of one team member whose performance you want to improve.

Whether it's one sticky issue that's bugging you or just they're general lack of fire on the project they're working on.

Use the seven step strategy I showed you earlier to hold a coaching session with them.

If you do it right, and are willing to make mistakes in order to improve, you'll start to see results.

All you need to do is take that first step.

And unlock the inner rock star in your team.

Your Free Book

As a way of saying *thanks* for your purchase, I'm offering a free report that's exclusive to my book and my newsletter readers.

In *7 Questions To Build Trust*, you'll discover a ladder of questions that will gain the lasting trust of your team member.

Using these questions you can then follow up to have a truly effective coaching session which will motivate your team like never before.

>>> Go To The Link Below To Claim Your Free Book <<<

www.icaruspublishing.theheasman.com/coaching

References

[1] http://psycnet.apa.org/journals/abn/52/3/304/

[2] https://hbr.org/2014/06/the-simplest-way-to-build-trust/

[3] http://boss.blogs.nytimes.com/2014/03/11/the-surprisingly-large-cost-of-telling-small-lies/

[4] http://sethgodin.typepad.com/seths_blog/2013/02/how-to-listen.html

[5] http://www.wsj.com/articles/tuning-in-how-to-listen-better-1406070727

www.ingramcontent.com/pod-product-compliance
Lightning Source LLC
Chambersburg PA
CBHW070941180526
45168CB00003B/1136